In 1966, Ronnie shot dead a member of a rival gang in The Blind Beggar Pub. Ronnie  also commit a murder. In 1967 ment flat. Although no witn ed by "Nipper" Read of Scotland Krays and Firm members in May ornell's murder spoke out; sever ence", testifying about McVitie's l was that they committed the y trial (then the longest and most expensive criminal trial in British history) ended at the Old Bailey. Ronnie was found guilty of the murder of Cornell and Reggie was found guilty of the murder of McVitie. The Twins were both sentenced to life imprisonment, with a recommendation that they each serve a minimum of 30 years. Charlie and 6 other Firm members were also sentenced.

Despite being jailed, the Twins kept a hold on peoples' imagination – with books, films, documentaries, marriages in prison (Reggie married once and Ronnie married twice) and visits by celebrities, they built up their own celebrity status. Many people felt their sentences had been unduly harsh.

The Kray brothers are now dead: Ronnie had served 26 years, when he died, aged 61, of a heart attack in March 1995. He had been certified insane 16 years before. **Charlie**, in prison again for drug smuggling, died from heart failure, in April 2000, aged 73. In August 2000, **Reggie** was released from prison on compassionate grounds (he had terminal cancer) – he had served 31 years. He died in his sleep in October 2000, aged 66. Their deaths and traditional funerals received huge media attention; Ronnie's was the grandest – the whole of the East End came to a standstill for his funeral. It was estimated that 40 to 50 thousand people lined the streets to see the procession – a number only surpassed in the last century by those who gathered for the funerals of Sir Winston Churchill and Princess Diana. This demonstrated and confirmed the popularity of the Twins, ensuring their place in East End folklore. When Reggie died, it was the end of an era. The East End of London would never be the same again – and the Krays had truly passed into legend – something of which they would heartily approve.

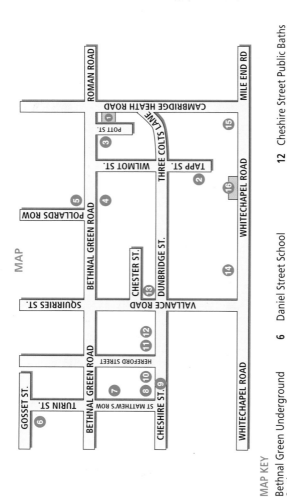

MAP

MAP KEY

1 Bethnal Green Underground Station
2 The Lion Public House
3 W English and Son Funeral Directors
4 Pellici's Café

6 Daniel Street School
7 St Matthew's Church
8 The Carpenters' Arms Public House
9 Cheshire Street

12 Cheshire Street Public Baths
13 Site of 178 Vallance Road
14 The Grave Maurice Public House
15 The Blind Beggar Public House

OPENING TIMES

Pellici's Café:	Open Monday – Saturday; closed Sunday
St Matthew's Church:	Various.
The Carpenters' Arms Pub:	Mon. – Fri., 6.00 pm – 11.00 pm; Sat., 8.00 pm – 11.00 pm; Sun., 8.00 am – 10.30 pm
The Grave Maurice Pub:	Mon. – Sat., 11.00 am – 11.00 pm; Sun., 12.00 noon – 11.00 pm
The Blind Beggar Pub:	Mon. – Sat., 11.00 am – 11.00 pm; Sun., 12.00 noon – 10.30 pm

START OF THE WALK

Directions: Start this Walk at Bethnal Green Underground Station ❶, which is on the Central Line. Exit the ticket barriers and continue to walk directly ahead. Exit via the staircase on the left and, when at street level, continue straight ahead. Walk down Cambridge Heath Road, keeping on the right. Turn right into the third road on the right, which is called Three Colts Lane. Continue along on the left, under the railway bridge and follow the road as it bends left, until you reach Bethnal Green Railway Station. Turn left down Tapp Street, which is just before the Station. Keeping on the right, walk under the railway arch and, immediately on the right, at N° 8 Tapp Street, is the building, which was The Lion Public House ❷

The Lion Public House: This Pub was known locally as "The Widow's" or "Madge's", after the widowed landlady, Madge. It was a typical East End backstreet pub – secluded and a perfect meeting place for the Krays. On the evening of 9 March 1966, the Twins and some of the Firm were drinking here. A member of Ronnie's "little information service" (boys who he paid to spy and inform him about other gangs) told him that George Cornell was drinking at The Blind Beggar Pub ❶❺ – in Kray territory!

A dangerous and deadly feud had grown between the Krays and a South London gang, the Richardsons, of whom Cornell was a member. The Twins believed that the Richardsons had been trying to kill them – one evening, just

after the Twins had left The Widow's, shots were fired at the Pub windows fr[...]
a moving car; later, a man, who looked like Ronnie, was knocked down by a [...]
as he walked along the pavement in Vallance Road. Before this feud could rea[...]
a climax, the Richardsons got involved in a gunfight with another gang, o[...]
March 1966, at Mr Smith's Club in Catford. During this "battle", a friend of t[...]
Krays was shot dead. All the important members of the Richardsons, exce[...]
Cornell, ended up in hospital, with a police guard, or in custody. With th[...]
rivals destroyed, the Krays could have ruled London, with no other gang able [...]
challenge their power. Ronnie, however, wanted revenge for his friend's dea[...]
the previous day, and for all the trouble the Richardsons had started. Corr[...]
was the ideal target, as he had also incurred Ronnie's wrath by badmouthi[...]
the Krays, even apparently calling Ronnie a "fat poof".

Taking two members of the Firm with him – Ian Barrie to accompany him a[...]
John Dickson to drive the car – Ronnie collected his pistol and set off for T[...]
Blind Beggar, where he shot George Cornell dead. After the shooting, Ron[...]
and Barrie left The Blind Beggar, got into the car waiting outside and Dicks[...]
drove them back to The Widow's. As they drove to the Pub, they could hear t[...]
sound of police car sirens.

Apparently, Ronnie arrived back at The Widow's in a pleased and excited mo[...]
he told Reggie first and then the others, about what he had done. T[...]
customers in The Widow's began to leave, as they heard about the shooti[...]
because they did not want to get involved. The Firm members also left to go [...]
a pub in Walthamstow, about 6 miles away. Ronnie changed his clothes a[...]
went upstairs to listen to a BBC news broadcast about the killing on the rad[...]

*Directions: Retrace your steps, going back under the railway arch to Beth[...]
Green Railway Station. Cross the road at the zebra crossing and walk dire[...]
ahead down Wilmot Street, on the right hand side. Continue to the end of t[...]
road to Bethnal Green Road. Turn right and walk along until you reach [...]
English and Son Funeral Directors ❸, which is on the corner of Pott Street, t[...]
second street on the right.*

W English and Son Funeral Directors: This local funeral parlour handled t[...]
funeral arrangements for all three Kray brothers. The body of each brother [...]
in the Chapel of Rest at this parlour, before being taken to St Matthew's Chu[...]
❼, where the funeral services took place.

Despite the poverty in the East End when the Krays were young, funerals were grand events – the Twins never forgot this, and they ensured that they and their family members each received a traditional send off.

Ronnie was the first of the brothers to die (in 1995) and his funeral was the largest of the three. The funeral was arranged by Reggie and Charlie and was said to have cost £10,000. The funeral cortege started from the Chapel of Rest here. Flowers lay on the pavement outside and people crowded the streets and rooftops surrounding the area. There were hundreds of wreaths, sent by family, friends (including Barbara Windsor and Roger Daltrey), local boxing clubs and some from strangers; but the largest were from Reggie and formed the words: "The Other Half of Me" and "The Kray Twins".

As befitting tradition, the head undertaker (dressed in black and wearing a silk top hat) walked at the head of the procession. Ronnie's coffin was inside a Victorian glass–sided carriage. The carriage, decorated with wreaths, was pulled by six black horses, with black plumes on their heads. The undertakers' colleagues walked by the sides of the carriage.

Following the carriage, as it went along Bethnal Green Road, was a car carrying Reggie. (Reggie, still serving his life sentence for murder, was allowed to attend by the prison authorities, but was accompanied by four warders, one of who was handcuffed to him. The last time Reggie had been allowed out of prison was in 1983 for Violet's funeral, which Ronnie had also attended.) 24 limousines followed Reggie's car. Bethnal Green Road was lined with thousands of people, some shouting "*Free Reggie Now!*" as the procession made the short journey to the Church.

In April 2000, Reggie was again released from prison, to attend brother Charlie's funeral. In October of the same year, Reggie, the last Kray Twin, also died. In contrast to the media interest in Ronnie's funeral, the storm over the arrangements for Reggie's funeral (made by himself in his last days and his second wife, Roberta) caused almost as much press coverage as the ceremony itself. Much publicity was also given to the security guards (estimates of their numbers ranged from 100–400) – dressed in long black overcoats with red armbands and wearing "RKF" (Reg Kray Funeral) lapel badges – who were used to line the route and hold back the crowds. Among the hundreds of wreaths, were those that spelt: "Legend", "Free at Last", "Hero" and "Reunited at Last".

Directions: *Return to Wilmot Street and then continue down Bethnal Gre* *Road, keeping on the left. Stop at N° 332, which is opposite a church and Pellici's Café* ➍*. This is a good place to stop off for some refreshment.*

Pellici's Café: This Café, which has stood on this site for over 100 years, was o of the Twins' regular hangouts, both when they were in their teens and lat when they had become notorious in the area.

During the 1950s, Pellici's was a popular meeting place for local youths, as it v close to the Mansford Mixed Youth Club. One Saturday afternoon in 1950, t Twins were standing outside the Café with a few friends. A young policema PC Baynton, decided the boys were obstructing the pavement, and so he shov Ronnie in the back to move him on. Ronnie immediately retaliated, a punched the policeman in the mouth. The other boys ran off, but two oth policemen, who drew up in a police car, caught Ronnie. Ronnie was taken ba to the police station, where he claimed he was beaten up by police officers his cell. When Ronnie arrived home, badly bruised, he is said to have said:
"The bastards could only do me in numbers... There were about six of the hitting me, but I got a few punches in myself." (Ronnie Kray by L O'Leary)

Reggie did not get a chance to help at the time, so he walked back do Bethnal Green Road looking for PC Baynton. When Reggie found him, he a punched him in the mouth!

The Twins were charged with assault. Ronnie pleaded provocation a Reggie said he had acted in Ronnie's defence. Father Hetherington, then vi of St James's Church ➎, spoke for the boys at the magistrates' court. Althou the Twins only got put on probation, this was bad publicity for th boxing careers.

Directions: *Opposite Pellici's Café, is a building that resembles a church; this w St James the Great Church* ➎*. Cross the road to the Church at a safe place.*

St James the Great Church: Today, the Church has closed for business a although the exterior, with its high red spire, has not changed, the interior h been redeveloped into some exclusive flats. In 1965, this Church was the ven for the East End's "marriage of the year", when Reggie Kray married Fran Shea on 19 April.

Reggie asked Father Hetherington (vicar of the Church when the Twins were young) to perform the ceremony. Father Hetherington had also run a youth club in the Bethnal Green Road, which the Twins had attended, and was an old friend of theirs; he had often spoken up for the Twins when they were in trouble:

"They were extremely kind boys and would do anything for me except actually come to church." (The Profession of Violence, by John Pearson)

This time, however, Father Hetherington would not be involved, because, he said (without explanation) he did not think the wedding should take place. The current vicar of St James's performed the ceremony instead.

Frances, who was aged 21, was dressed in white, in a full-length dress. Ronnie was the best man and there were 200 guests. Many famous boxers (such as Terry Allen, Terry Spinks, and Ted "Kid" Lewis) attended the wedding, as well as many celebrities. Telegrams were received from Judy Garland, Barbara Windsor, Lord Boothby and others. David Bailey was the photographer. The couple were driven to the wedding reception at the Finsbury Park Hotel in a maroon Rolls Royce.

Unfortunately, the marriage soon ran into problems, causing the couple to separate after only eight weeks. Frances began to suffer from depression. Francis had apparently told Reggie, when they were courting, that she did not think she would live long after her 21st birthday. This premonition turned out to be true – after two suicide attempts, on 7 June 1967, Frances was found dead (aged only 23), from an overdose of barbiturates. A verdict of suicide was recorded. Reggie was devastated:

"I've only ever loved – and I mean really loved – two women in my whole life. And I've lost them both. One was my mother and the other was my wife Frances. Ironically, it was Frances who died first."

(Reg & Ron Kray: Our Story, by Fred Dinenage – 1988)

Tragically, two years after the wedding, this Church was used for the bride's funeral. The Krays organised a grand funeral, just as they had organised the grand wedding. Father Hetherington agreed to take the service. There were 10 black limousines for the mourners and many wreaths, including one from Ronnie (who did not attend as he was on the run from the police at the time) and three from Reggie.

There was conflict between Frances' parents, the Sheas, and Reggie over t
arrangements (each blamed the other for the girl's death). In the end, t
funeral took place in the name of "Frances Shea, otherwise Kray". Frances w
buried in her wedding dress at Chingford Cemetery, although the She
arranged for her to be dressed in a slip and stockings, as they apparen
wanted to avoid the dress touching her skin as much as possible. Reggie a
wanted Frances to be buried with her wedding ring; the Sheas, however, cla
they switched the ring before the burial.

Directions: Continue past the Church, crossing Pollards Row and continue do
Bethnal Green Road on the right hand side. Continue for approx. 600 m, ur
you arrive at Turin Street. Turn right into Turin Street and keep on the left. W
to the end of Turin Street and on the left is the Bethnal Green Centre for Sp
and the Performing Arts; in the 1940s and 50s, this was Daniel Street School

Daniel Street School: The Kray Twins were 11, when they started at this Scho
Here, there was an incident, in which Reggie got a black eye, when he got ir
a fight with an older boy. This made Reggie realise that, although he wa
"good scrapper", he needed to learn about the finer techniques of boxing.
asked his elder brother, Charlie, who was boxing in the Royal Navy at the tin
to teach him. Charlie taught both the Twins. Violet let them use the upsta
front bedroom at home as a training room. For a punchbag, they stuffed o
of Charlie's Navy kitbags full of rags and old clothes; they hung this from t
ceiling and attached it to the floor with a meat hook. One night, a dru
Charlie Snr, crept into the room and impaled his foot on the hook, much
everyone else's amusement. The Twins used their homemade gym for sparri
and chatting to their friends until 1949, when Violet let son, Charlie, and
new wife move into it.

The Twins claimed to be happy at this School; even though it was never qu
exciting enough, they were encouraged to box and play football. One of th
teachers at the School, Bill Evans, is quoted as saying that the Kray Twins we
"the salt of the earth. Never the slightest bother as long as you knew how
handle them." (Reg & Ron Kray: Our Story, by Fred Dinenage)

It was at this School that the Twins often tricked and confused the teachers
pretending to be one another. They were to use this stunt many times in t
future to escape trouble with the Army and the Law (including when Ronn

escaped from Long Grove Mental Hospital, to where he had been transferred from prison, when he was certified insane in 1958).

Directions: Walk back down Turin Street and cross Bethnal Green Road at the zebra crossing. Continue directly ahead into St Matthew's Row. On the left you will see St Matthew's Church **7**

St Matthew's Church: The funeral services of all three Kray brothers, and also of their mother, were held at this Church.

When Ronnie died in March 1995, brothers Reggie and Charlie, issued an open invitation for people to attend the service at this Church. Charlie was one of the six pallbearers, who carried Ronnie's coffin (made of dark oak, with golden handles) into the Church. Reggie, on release from prison, was handcuffed to a warder throughout the service. The Church was completely packed – with all 200 seats taken and people standing at the back and in the aisles. Crowds of people, who had not been able to join the service, were outside the Church. The service began with a tape of Frank Sinatra's "My Way". Messages, including the following from Reggie, were read out:

"My brother Ron is now free and at peace. Ron had great humour, a vicious temper, was kind and generous. ... " (Ronnie Kray by Laurie O'Leary)

The service ended with the song, "I Will Always Love You", by Whitney Houston. Many family members and friends felt that Reggie was destroyed when Ronnie died.

Ronnie's body was taken to Chingford Mount Cemetery in Essex, a few miles away, where he was buried beside the graves of his mother and father. The bodies of brothers, Charlie and Reggie, were later also buried in this family plot. (Although Ronnie's body was buried that day, it later materialised that his brain had not been buried at that time. Home Office Chiefs had apparently secretly, and without the family's permission, ordered the removal of Ronnie's brain before the funeral, so that they could use it for research into criminal behaviour. Consequently, a second funeral had to be held a few months later to bury Ronnie's brain.)

When Charlie died in April 2000, his funeral was much more low-key than Ronnie's. Despite this, the Church was packed to capacity, with hundreds more

outside. Press accounts said the congregation was not allowed into the Churc
until Reggie, handcuffed to a prison officer, had arrived, and that, when insid
they lined up to kiss him, in "Mafia style".

When Reggie, the last Kray brother, died in a Hotel near Norwich, on 1 Octob
2000, some of his old friends, who were at his bedside, said that Reggie aske
them to be his pallbearers. However, Reggie's second wife, Roberta (whom h
married while he was in prison in 1997) maintained that Reggie had not wante
"any gangster friends" as pallbearers. Roberta is also said to have upset mar
of Reggie's older friends by not inviting them to the funeral. (This service w
by invitation only). Many other older friends did not come to the Church as
mark of protest. Some claimed that Roberta was trying to stop the funeral fro
being a gangland spectacle like the funerals of his brothers. As a result of all th
bad feeling, several seats in the Church remained empty.

The congregation cheered and clapped as the coffin was brought into th
Church. The service centered on Reggie as a reformed Christian. Reggi
solicitor gave an address, in which he said that: *"Reg was an icon of the 20
century."* The coffin left the Church to Frank Sinatra's, "My Way" (also playe
at Ronnie's funeral). As the cortege left for the Cemetery, applause burst o
and people shouted: "Goodbye, Reggie!"

*Directions: Exit the Church via the churchyard gate and turn left. Contin
down St Matthew's Row to the end of the street and, on the left, on the corn
is The Carpenters' Arms Public House* **8**

The Carpenters' Arms Public House: This small pub, hidden away in the ba
streets, was known well to the Twins, being just around the corner fro
their home.

The Twins bought the Pub in the autumn of 1967. It was a difficult time
them – George Cornell had been murdered, Frank Mitchell (the "Mad Axema
whom the Twins had helped escape from Dartmoor Prison) had disappeare
there was trouble in the Firm and Frances had recently died. Also, they had r
been able to keep running their clubs. They needed their own safe place,
which to drink, and from where they could issue orders to the Firm; this lo
pub, with its narrow bar and one doorway to the road, fitted the bill perfec
No one could get into the Pub unobserved. The Twins decorated the Pub w

red–striped Regency wallpaper and red velvet seats, turning it into a sort of private club for themselves. It became one of their favourite places in the 1960s.

Parties for the Firm were sometimes held here at weekends. Women would attend these occasions, the dress code was formal and drinks were "on the house". Such a party took place here on 28 October 1967. The Twins' mother, Violet, was present that night. Ronnie was, apparently, in a strange and dangerous mood and most people avoided him. The Twins talked together and, after that, Reggie began drinking heavily. At closing time, Reggie, drunk and aggressive, made off hurriedly.

The reason for the Twins' menacing behaviour was that they had decided that Jack "the Hat" McVitie (named because he always wore a hat to cover up his bald patch) had to be taught a lesson. McVitie had cheated the Twins over some business and ignored warnings; he then took money to kill someone for them, but did not carry out the murder. He refused to repay the money and caused trouble in clubs of their friends. The night before, he had staggered, drunk, into the Regency Club in North London and, waving a sawn–off shotgun, threatened to kill the Krays.

Reggie left the Carpenters' Arms to go to the Regency (where he thought McVitie was) apparently intending to shoot him in the head, with his .32 automatic gun, just as Ronnie had shot Cornell. But McVitie was not at the Club. Reggie did not give up. McVitie was found and invited by the Lambrianou brothers (who needed to prove their loyalty, in order to join the Firm) to a party in a basement flat in Stoke Newington. Drunk and high on drugs, he was brought to the flat just after midnight.

The Twins and some of the Firm were waiting. According to accounts given to the police, Reggie tried to shoot McVitie in the head, but his gun jammed. McVitie almost escaped through the window, but only succeeded in losing his hat. McVitie begged for mercy, but Reggie, egged on by Ronnie (*"Kill him, Reg. Do him."* – *The Profession of Violence, by John Pearson*), who was holding back the victim's arms, stabbed McVitie in the face with a carving knife. He then stabbed his body and chest and finally impaled him to the floor by stabbing him through his throat. The Twins left the flat. The Firm members mopped up the blood and took the body away. Within a couple of days the room was redecorated, with new furniture. The body of McVitie was never found.

Directions: *Exit the Pub onto Cheshire Street* **9** *. (There is a "bric–a–br* *market in this Street on Sunday mornings).*

Cheshire Street: In the Twins' autobiography (Reg & Ron Kray: Our Story, Fred Dinenage), Ronnie recalls how, during the War, his Grandad Lee argu with one of Mosley's Blackshirts in this Street, when the Fascist was be derogatory about the Jews.

Reggie also recalls an incident in this Street. When he was only 8, he a friend, Alf (aged about 9), who helped the local bread delivery m Alf was paid by the man to start up the engine of his van and load the bre One day, Reggie and Alf were in the van, when Alf turned on the ignition then put the van into gear as a joke. To their horror, the van sped backwa resulting in a 6 year–old boy being crushed to death between the van and air–raid shelter behind them. There was blood everywhere. The delivery r made the boys promise not to tell anyone that Alf had started the engine the boys only admitted to playing with the gears. As a result, there a verdict of "accidental death" and the delivery man did not lose his j However, it also meant that the victim's family could not claim compensat from the bread company. Reggie was truly upset by the incident, which he l recalled as a bad omen – made worse for him by the fact that the dead boy also a twin.

In January 1965, "Ginger" Marks was shot dead by gunmen in a moving ca he walked along this Street at night. His body was dragged off in the car. S blood, a used cartridge and Marks' black, horn–rimmed glasses were left on pavement. There was also a bullet hole in the wall. Marks' body was ne found. Ronnie claimed that George Cornell had boasted to him that he killed Marks; so, when Ronnie killed Cornell, he was *"only killing a kil* (My Story by Ron Kray).

Directions: *Directly next door to the Pub is Wood Close School* **10**

Wood Close School: This was the Twins' primary school. School began ag after being closed due to the bombing in the War, when the Twins were 8 y old. The boys' small mongrel dog, which they called "Lassie", would come meet them from here. The Twins were happy at this School, which t attended until they were 11.

Directions: Continue past Wood Close School, crossing Hereford Street and shortly on the left you arrive at Repton Amateur Boxing Club **11**, now called Repton Boys' Club.

Repton Amateur Boxing Club: During their early teens, the Twins started to train in boxing clubs, such as this famous Club and the Webbe Club Gym. Reggie was the more promising of the Twins, who both won many amateur titles, and later turned professional, aged 17.

Ronnie, aged 15, was in the Club one night, when a film director was looking for extras for a film, "The Magic Box", being made at Ealing Studios. Ronnie was thrilled to take part and recalled this, years later. *(My Story by Ron Kray)*.

Although the Twins decided not to pursue careers in boxing, they retained their love of the sport and its glamour. When this Club put on a special show in 1961, "local businessman Ronald Kray" donated the trophies. The local newspaper described the Twins' generosity (they also helped by buying tickets) and included a photo of Ronnie with Billy Walker, the boxer. Celebrities, including Barbara Windsor, were guests at the show.

Through their boxing connections, and later, through the American Mafia (who controlled sports celebrities at the time) the Krays met many world champion boxers including Rocky Graziano, Joe Louis, Sonny Liston and Freddie Mills. They, and other celebrities, would go to the Clubs, which the Twins owned.

Directions: Immediately next door to the Repton Amateur Boxing Club are the Cheshire Street Public Baths **12**

Cheshire Street Public Baths: The Krays' home, as most houses in the area, did not have a bathroom. People had to wash in the yard, in a tin bath full of water heated by fuel (wood and coal). So, it was easier to go to these communal public baths and they were very popular. Although most locals only came once a week, the Twins were there every day. The boys and their friends knew the attendants and did not have to queue.

After the Twins' arrest in 1968, the police questioned one of the attendants about the Firm. The police, apparently, were particularly interested in the furnace, used to heat the water for the baths – they thought that some of the

bodies connected to the Kray case may have been disposed of in this. They co
not, however, find any evidence.

There are many other theories, some apparently made up by Ronnie hims
about what happened to the various missing bodies connected to the Kra
including that the bodies were concreted into the foundations of a motorv
or office block, made into pig food or buried in Epping Forest. One of the m
plausible, however, was that the Krays had the help of a local undertake
there were stories about how the Twins paid for special cremations and a
how extra bodies were placed inside, (already occupied) coffins, just before
lids were screwed down.

Today, the building which housed the public baths, is private property.

*Directions: Continue, on the left hand side, to the end of the street, until
arrive at the junction with Vallance Road. Turn left and cross Vallance Roac
the zebra crossing. Turn right, when on the other side of the road. Cross Che.
Street and, immediately on your left, is a block of six houses; this was the site
178 Vallance Road* **13**

178 Vallance Road: The Krays' family home once stood exactly on the s
where the plaque (commemorating the opening of the flats), is situated too
The Kray family moved here in 1939, just before the outbreak of the 2nd W
War, as Violet wanted to be near her family, the Lees. The locals called this p
of Vallance Road "Lee Street" – Violet's parents lived a few doors away,
brother had a café on the opposite side of the street and her sisters, May
Rose (Ronnie's favourite aunt, who was "as tough as any man") both lived c
by. When Ronnie asked Rose why his eyebrows went right across his nose
joined in the middle, she replied:

"It means you were born to hang, Ronnie love." *(My Story by Ron Kray)*

178 Vallance Road (second in a row of 4 Victorian terraced houses) had
storeys, no bathroom and an outside toilet in the back yard, where the fa
kept chickens. The house shook, day and night, as trains going in and ou
Liverpool Street Station, roared past the end of the yard.

The Twins shared the upstairs back bedroom, which overlooked the rail
yard. Reggie would listen to the sounds of horns, whistles and shunting

trucks from this yard and, inspired by his Grandad Lee's stories, imagine that he would become a great boxer. The Twins also loved to listen from the window to their beloved mother singing in the backyard, as she hung out the washing.

When the War started, this area was constantly bombed, as German bombers aimed at the main railway lines. Over 10,000 homes in Bethnal Green were destroyed during the War. Because of the Blitz, the schools were closed, and the boys played in the back streets and in nearby ruins of bombed houses. The Twins had their own gang and always seemed to be fighting. During the bombing raids, the twins would take shelter, with hundreds of others, in air raid shelters under the railway arches, which are still there today (opposite). Grandad Lee would put on shows to entertain the people and there would be music and dancing. Most raids took place at night, and the Twins would often stand in the blacked out street, outside their home, staring up at the sky as huge searchlights searched for the bombers. At that time, this part of Vallance Road became known as "Deserters' Corner", because so many of the men who lived in this area (including Charlie Snr) had ignored their call-up papers or deserted from the Army. When the police came looking for Charlie, the Twins lied to help him, learning early that the police were the enemy.

Later, when the Twins became more notorious, the family home became the Headquarters of the Kray Empire. Ronnie, "The Colonel", was obsessed with firearms (he got his first gun when he was 16); his collection included revolvers of varying calibres and sawn-off shotguns – most of these were hidden under the floorboards. Ronnie also had other kinds of weapons, including cavalry sabres, knives and bayonets, he would sharpen his swords and knives on a big grindstone in the yard. The house became known as "Fort Vallance".

The Twins continued to use the house well into their adult life for operations and also as a place of sanctuary, even when they had moved out. Violet Kray finally left 178 Vallance Road in 1967, when she moved to a new council flat in Braithwaite House in Shoreditch.

Directions: Continue past 178 Vallance Road. Cross Dunbridge Street and continue under the railway bridge on the left hand side. Continue to the very end of Vallance Road, until you arrive at Whitechapel Road. Turn left, continue approx. 200 m on the left hand side, until you arrive at The Grave Maurice Public House **14** *, which is just after N° 267 Whitechapel Road.*

The Grave Maurice Public House: This Pub was Ronnie's local. He would sit the far end of the Pub, with his back to the wall, so he could see the ma entrance. The Grave Maurice is still, today, a traditional East End pub. Notice t pictures of the Krays above the bar.

Ronnie is said to have resolved a dispute between George Cornell and "Ging Marks here. However, after Marks left the Pub, Cornell apparently told Ron that he hated Marks and he wanted to blow his head off (see **9**). Reggie or brought Christine Keeler, the prostitute involved in the Profumo scanc to this Pub.

When "Nipper" Read first came to the East End, in the early 1960s, to work the case against the Krays, he went, unnoticed, for a quiet drink in the Gr Maurice, so that he could observe the Twins at close hand.

Directions: Exit the Grave Maurice and turn left, continuing along Whitecha Road, past Whitechapel Underground Station. Approx. 100 m after Underground Station, on the left, is one of London's most famous pubs – 7 Blind Beggar Public House **15**

The Blind Beggar Public House: This Pub will always be associated with killing of George Cornell in the main bar, by Ronnie Kray. At that time, The Bl Beggar was often frequented by criminals. Today, however, this friendly p offers a relaxed atmosphere for all the family, helpful staff and provides gc pub food.

On the evening of 9 March 1966, Ronnie walked into the Pub, with Ian Bar (They had just come from The Lion **2**) There were not many people in The Bl Beggar, and the barmaid had just put a record on the jukebox – "The Sun A Gonna Shine Anymore", by the Walker Brothers.

Ronnie and Barrie walked up to Cornell, who was in the saloon bar, sitting o stool by the end of the bar with a couple of friends. When he saw Ronn Cornell said: *"Well, look who's here."* Ronnie said nothing, but took out 9–mm Mauser automatic pistol, which he had carried into the Pub in shoulder holster, and shot Cornell in the forehead. Cornell fell off his stoc there was blood everywhere. Barrie, also armed, fired two shots into the ceili Everyone else ran for cover, except an old man who remained sitting at a ta